Soaring on Purpose:
A Devotional for Intentional Living

Jonathan Leysath

Soaring on Purpose: A Devotional for Intentional Living

Copyright © 2025 Jonathan Leysath
Leysath Literary Management, LLC
ISBN: 9798992862201
Publisher: Rise2Write Publishing LLC
All rights reserved. No part of this publication may be reproduced, stored in a retrieval system, or transmitted in any form or by any means for example, electronic, photocopy, or records without prior written permission. The only exceptions are brief quotations in printed reviews.
Scripture quotations are taken from the Holy Bible, New King James Version®. Copyright © 1982 by Thomas Nelson. Used by permission. All rights reserved.
For information about custom editions, special sales, premium, and bulk purchases, please contact:
authorjonathanleysath@gmail.com
rise2write@gmail.com
www.rise2write.com

DEDICATION

In memory of Annie Williams McManus and Mable Simmons Leysath, my grandmothers who taught me that there was nothing prayer couldn't fix.

Table of Contents

INTRODUCTION 9
PART 1 IF IT HAPPENS, IT HAPPENS............................11
DAY 1: BRING YOUR PURPOSE TO LIFE 13
DAY 2: RELATIONSHIPS 15
DAY 3: INTENTIONAL WAITING 17
DAY 4: PREPARING YOUR HEART FOR GOD'S WILL 21
DAY 5: EMBRACING YOUR MIND..................................23
PART 2: WHY JUST BEING, ISN'T ENOUGH- GOD WANTS MORE..25
DAY 6: UNDERSTANDING YOUR PURPOSE IN CHRIST........27
DAY 7: FAITH IN MOTION 29
DAY 8: NO LONGER BEING PASSIVE BUT PURPOSEFUL......31
DAY 9: TRUSTING GOD WHILE BEING YOU 33
DAY 10: YOUR ROLE IN GOD'S PLAN 35
PART 3: A TIME TO PIVOT AND A TIME TO MOVE 37
DAY 11: OVERCOMING FEAR...39
DAY 12: KNOWING WHEN IT IS TIME TO SHIFT 41
DAY 13: THE COURAGE TO PIVOT 43
DAY 14: SEEKING GOD'S GUIDANCE IN UNCERTAINTY.....45
DAY 15: SEEKING STRENGTH DURING TRANSITION 47
PART 4: BE INTENTIONAL WITH BEING THERE FOR YOUR LOVED ONES, FRIENDS, COLLEAGUES. 49
DAY 16: SHOW UP FOR THOSE WE CARE ABOUT.....51
DAY 17: THE GIFT OF BEING PRESENT 53
DAY 18: INTENTIONAL PRAYERS FOR YOUR LOVED ONES 55
DAY 19: SPEAKING LIFE INTO YOUR LOVED ONES 57
DAY 20: BEING INTENTIONAL WITH CREATING LASTING MEMORIES 59

PART 5: BE INTENTIONAL WITH YOUR FAITH WALK 61

DAY 21: FAITH IN UNCERTAINTY 63

DAY 22: YOU REAP WHAT YOU SOW 65

DAY 23: UNDERSTANDING TRUE INVESTMENTS 67

DAY 24: INTENTIONAL IN EVERYDAY DECISIONS 69

DAY 25: GOD'S FAITHFULNESS 71

PART 6: THERE IS POWER IN BEING PURPOSEFUL, SHOW UP ON PURPOSE 73

DAY 26: BUILDING TRUST IN YOUR JOURNEY 75

DAY 27: SETTING SPIRITUAL GOALS 79

DAY 28: THE CURSE OF PROCRASTINATION 80

DAY 29: PRIORITIZING SPIRITUAL GROWTH OVER TEMPORARY PLEASURES 83

DAY 30: IDENTIFYING YOUR GIFTS 85

PART 7: YOU INVEST IN WHAT WILL BE FRUITFUL, NOT IN WHAT YOU LOVE 87

DAY 31: BEING PURPOSEFUL 89

DAY 32: ALIGNING ACTIONS WITH PURPOSE 91

DAY 33: CREATING A PURPOSE-DRIVEN ENVIRONMENT ..93

DAY 34: THE IMPORTANCE OF QUALITY TIME 95

DAY 35: STAY FOCUSED 97

PART 8: BE INTENTIONAL WITH YOUR WALK IN CHRIST 99

DAY 36: INTENTIONAL LIVING 101

DAY 37: DAILY SURRENDER 103

DAY 38: CHRIST AT THE CENTER OF YOUR LIFE 105

DAY 39: FINDING INTENTIONAL JOY IN TODAY 107

DAY 40: TRUSTING GOD TO LEAD IN NEW DIRECTIONS .109

ACKNOWLEDGMENTS 111

ABOUT JONATHAN LEYSATH 113

INTRODUCTION

It's November 2, 2019, and I was working in our apartment when God inspired me. I then posted something on my Facebook page. Here's what it said:

"Spent the morning setting up devices for customers. I haven't spent a lot of attention to this part of the business, and it's been intentional. I'm learning every day that realignments are important for a properly balanced life. Are you balanced or are you running around trying to make things happen? Pace yourself and be intentional in your life. You only have two, and this one will end without notice."

Five years later, everywhere I turned, I heard the word "Intention" in some form or another. I would be listening to something, watching television, and, more oddly, just having conversations. I started applying it to my life and began to see improvements, not just for me but for my family as well. We moved from living in a two-bedroom apartment that was so damaged you could see directly through the sheetrock to the outside. In that apartment, we managed three businesses, worked a full-time job, and planted a church that required us to set up and break down every Sunday. If you recall, 2019 was our last year before COVID. Something had to change.

We became very intentional, and God blessed us in amazing ways. We prioritized our work with the church, family, and businesses, but little things surprised us. We researched, planned, prayed, and focused intently. Since then, God blessed us by helping us acquire a building for the church. We were planting and transitioning two businesses to give us time to focus on one that surpassed the combined revenues of all three in just one year. We watched our newly constructed Florida home come to life from the ground up, where we live today.

What I've come to understand is that God honors intentionality. You don't need to do a million things to please God; you just have to be faithful to what he has graced you.

As you engage with this devotional, I challenge you to explore deeply what God has given you and be intentional with every step and decision you make, and you will see God bless you. Remember, seeing the vision is not something you invoke, but writing the vision is! God may provide the vision, but it's your responsibility to write it!

PART 1 IF IT HAPPENS, IT HAPPENS

"The only way it happens is if you are intentional in your plans to make it happen."

DAY 1: BRING YOUR PURPOSE TO LIFE

Jeremiah 29:11: "For I know the thoughts that I think toward you, saith the LORD, thoughts of peace, and not of evil, to give you an expected end."

In this crazy world we call life, it's astonishing how often we wander around waiting for things to happen. How many times have you gone to the grocery store without a shopping list? What about when you feel like driving without a clue of where the car might stop? How often do we sit on the couch, remote control in hand, just scrolling? As we flip through channels, browsing the plethora of on-demand shows and movies or even the numerous streaming platforms we trick ourselves into subscribing to every month, we still can't find anything we actually want to watch. Isn't it remarkable how life lets us drift by without clear plans or intentions?

We often look for opportunities in our careers and businesses with the sole intention of making money. But what if I told you that what you planned for, and your purpose is more important than money? We subscribe to the notion of moving forward because we feel the need to be doing something. We continue to draft ideas and plans for our businesses. We work certain jobs perhaps because it's the family business. Some basketball players play the game simply because they've been surrounded by it their entire lives. Their parents played basketball, so they decided they would become basketball players. They want to be just like their dad or just like their mom. What happens when you chase your purpose instead of what feels familiar?

What if you were intentional about everything you did? Yes, I might be a plumber today, but I'm called to be a musician, so

I have to be intentional about practicing and improving. You can't decide to simply wake up and play a gig. You must be intentional every day to enhance your craft so that you can attract the attention of those who can help you get into position. You need to wake up and focus on being intentional with your practice, understanding music theory, knowing what people enjoy listening to, and learning how to adapt to the atmosphere in a room. This preparation is essential to be ready when opportunities arise.

There's a saying: "Stay ready so you don't have to Get ready!"

Prayer
Oh Father God in Heaven, as we prepare to bring purpose to our life, allow us to be able to bring intentionality into every facet of our life. We pray that as you strengthen us to be able to take on the skill of preparation, allow us to be able to prepare for the things that we can see while also preparing for the things that we cannot. As we become more intentional with our skills, with our practice, and even within our language we ask that you stand at the Forefront and guide us in every way. You have told us in your word that you know the thoughts that YOU think towards us and we are confident in that very fact. No matter how scared we are at times, we still trust the thoughts that you have towards us. It's for this reason we know that we can trust you to bring our dreams to reality. So while we are being intentional about planning, about practicing, we move with anticipation knowing that we are living a life that you ordain if we stay purposeful in every step of our day. In Jesus Name, Amen!

DAY 2: RELATIONSHIPS

1 John 4:20 KJV "If a man say, I love God, and hateth his brother, he is a liar: for he that loveth not his brother whom he hath seen, how can he love God whom he hath not seen?
1 John 4:21 And this commandment have we from him, That he who loveth God love his brother also."

Let's reflect on the relationships in your life. I understand that relationships are important. They're not just important because you like someone or were born into a particular family. They are essential to our existence because we need to connect with others to be effective. My wife and I have a special bond not just because we decided to get married one day, but because we started as friends. We were very intentional about spending time together. We didn't realize then, but understand now, that by spending time together, we would grow and learn from each other. We simply discovered each other's favorite colors, foods, and movies by enjoying each other's company. We just loved being around each other. Now, after so many years and countless routines of waking up, going to work, returning home, having dinner, watching a couple of TV shows, and going to sleep, only to start it all over again the next day, we can fall into a routine, and at some point, desire can diminish. In any relationship, you must be intentional about continuing to learn about the other person. Why? Just like them, you are also changing and evolving. You are not the same person you were ten years ago. It's crucial to intentionally learn who the person is becoming and not just who they are in the present moment.

One question: How are you being intentional about growing in your relationship with God?

Don't let your relationship with God happen passively. It thrives when both partners are committed to it together. He's nurturing it every day. You wake up to brand new mercies each day because He bestows them. Now, what are you doing?

Prayer
Oh Father God in Heaven, Help us not just to be receivers of a healthy relationship from our spiritual father but to also be givers. When the time comes for us to do and to give you something in return, help us to be able to do so with a willing heart. Help us to understand you more when we read your word and we call upon your name through prayer. In doing so, it will strengthen not only our relationship with you, but it will also help us to identify ourselves. While we are strengthening our relationship with you, help us to also reciprocate the same with our family, friends, and our loved ones. Ultimately, we want to become doers in our relationships and not just receivers.
In Jesus Name, Amen!

DAY 3: INTENTIONAL WAITING

John 5:7 KJV: "The impotent man answered him, Sir, I have no man, when the water is troubled, to put me into the pool: but while I am coming, another steppeth down before me."
John 5:8 KJV: "Jesus saith unto him, Rise, take up thy bed, and walk."
John 5:9 KJV: "And immediately the man was made whole, and took up his bed, and walked: and on the same day was the sabbath."

The saying "Timing is Everything" holds undeniable significance. However, what you do while waiting is even more important. In Jerusalem, there was a pool near the sheep market. What was remarkable about it was that, during a certain season, an angel would come and stir the water. Whoever entered first would be healed of any disease they had. Here, we find a man who had been infirm for 38 years. He had been coming to the pool, but no one was there to help him in. Every year, this miraculous event occurred, and people prepared for it.

What's fascinating is not just that they waited year-round for this to happen, but what they did during the wait. Many might look at this and say they did nothing all year but wait for this annual occurrence. I believe there was a different story for each of them. Can you imagine suffering all year and doing nothing except waiting for a moment? There are 31,536,000 seconds in a year, and to only be waiting for one of them to change your life seems unimaginable. Because of this perspective, I believe that many of them sought doctors, tried various remedies, and did everything they could to be healed. Everyone showed up knowing that this opportunity was certain. Unfortunately, the healing was only reserved for the first person to enter the pool.

For 38 years, the impotent man planned his return to the pool with every passing second. He knew he couldn't get there alone, so he had to ask for assistance to ensure he was on time and in place each year. Throughout those 38 years, he consistently showed up because he had FAITH.

When Jesus came he didn't ask him:
Why didn't you get in the pool?
Why didn't someone lift you?
Why did you even show up?

He simply asked the man.... Wilt though be made whole? The man's response was pretty common. He pretty much said, I'm trying! My question to you is, while you are waiting, what are you doing?

Many of us are just sitting around waiting for things to happen. Will you plan, show up, and give it your best, regardless of how talented your competition is or how stacked the deck is against you?

Just because you are waiting doesn't mean you should do nothing. You need to prepare for what's ahead, show up, and wait with expectation. Be intentional in your waiting! The impotent man didn't get healed the way he expected, but he was made whole after being intentional every year in his approach to showing up. It was in his "showing up" that allowed him to one day meet Jesus!

Prayer
Dear God, as we continue to wait on a move from you, grant us the strength to endure. Give us the strength to endure through adversity and through disappointment.

*Just as the scripture reminds us that when we are weak, that is when you are strong. So, as we wait on you with expectation and in action, helps to run to the end.
In Jesus Name, Amen!*

DAY 4: PREPARING YOUR HEART FOR GOD'S WILL

Proverbs 3:6 KJV "In all thy ways acknowledge him, and he shall direct thy paths."
Proverbs 16:9 KJV "A man's heart deviseth his way: but the LORD directeth his steps."

Webster defines "prepare" as to make ready beforehand for some purpose, use, or activity. Another important point is that "prepare" is a verb, indicating that it involves action. As people, it's easy to go through life waiting for God to take action or to think that if something is God's will over my life, it will simply happen. But what if God wants us to prepare for His will?

In fact, there is a scripture that tells us to acknowledge him in all our ways, and he will direct our paths. This was one of my aunt's favorite scriptures, and she would always remind us of it as we were growing up. Interestingly enough, my pastor always says a prayer of acknowledgment before any business meetings or decisions are made. We don't just pray and go about our day; we trust that any decisions made are left in God's hands to change or move them as He sees fit.

It's time to adopt the same approach in preparing our hearts for his will. We must acknowledge him, yes, but we must also ready our hearts for change. His thoughts are not our thoughts, nor are His plans. I'm the type who loves structure, and when someone changes things on me, I feel upset.

However, if I read that scripture and pray the prayer of acknowledgment, I shouldn't be upset when God alters the entire script. After all, it was a prayer requesting that God aligns our actions with his will, not that our actions become his will.

Prayer
God help us to stay in your will! While we seek opportunities of advancement, we dare not move outside of your will. Help us to keep our minds clear and our thoughts pure so that we have the capacity to hear your heart. Grant us with the heart to not be stubborn in our own ways to but to be flexible to yours. While we move with your authority, we pray that we stay humble that we always walk in the paths you set.
In Jesus Name, Amen!

DAY 5: EMBRACING YOUR MIND

Proverbs 19:21 KJV: "There are many devices in a man's heart; nevertheless the counsel of the LORD, that shall stand."

Scripture says he will keep you in perfect peace whose mind is stayed on him. I believe in having peace in my mind, but with how my life is set up, it can be hard to keep our minds on Christ, to be honest. However, I think many of us have interpreted that scripture incorrectly for years. I believe it means that intentionally creating narratives in your life centered around Christ helps keep your mind on him through things that reflect his nature. For example, three individuals enter a marriage: you, your spouse, and God. As you navigate through marriage, you do things that honor him. When planning a date night, your thoughts are essentially focused on how you are bringing honor to God, even while thinking about enjoying time with your wife.

The mistake we often make is focusing our minds on things that don't honor God and to which he is directly or indirectly connected. The more you direct your thoughts to him, the more you experience peace. Consider meditation or even prayer; these are the moments when we feel most at peace. However, reaching a state of peace requires intentional choices regarding every aspect of your life. The places you visit, your career, and your relationships, everything that fills your life starts to occupy your mind. If you desire peace, you must build a life centered on Christ.

Prayer
Oh Father God in Heaven, help us to keep our minds stayed on you. When storms arise in our life, help us to keep our minds stayed on you. When our enemies test us, help us to keep our minds on you. Grant us with the peace in our minds that surpasses all of our understanding. When our minds are stayed on you, we can embrace you within our hearts.
In Jesus Name, Amen!

PART 2: WHY JUST BEING, ISN'T ENOUGH- GOD WANTS MORE

"God, never let us settle in just being, but remind us that you require us to be Intentional with everything we do."

DAY 6: UNDERSTANDING YOUR PURPOSE IN CHRIST

Jeremiah 1:5 KJV "Before I formed thee in the belly I knew thee; and before thou camest forth out of the womb I sanctified thee, and I ordained thee a prophet unto the nations."

How many days have you wondered what your purpose in life is? How many times have you contemplated whether you are in the right role at your church, serving in the right ministry, or possibly even working at the right church? We sometimes spend too much time worrying about whether we are doing something right instead of actually doing it. I firmly believe that your purpose in life must be centered around Christ. The job you have, the boards you sit on, and yes, the ministries you are involved in. Understanding your purpose in Christ begins with knowing who you are and who He is. We recognize Him as Jireh - the Provider, Shalom - Peace, and much more. I encourage you to spend the next 24 hours discovering how others perceive you. Do they see you as an administrator, finance person, tech guru, or even an amazing creative?

Finding yourself means discovering who God wants you to be most of the time. After all, God doesn't save you to be someone else; He saves YOU. Scripture teaches us two things about gifts. They come without repentance (Romans 11:29) and will bring us before great men (Proverbs 18:16). Our gifts and calling are so powerful that great men will not only see them but also rely on them. The important part is that you don't lose sight of who God is in your life through your gift.

After all, you can understand your purpose in Christ while also losing Him (Matthew 7:23).

Prayer
Oh Father God in Heaven, thank you for choosing me and not giving up on me. I ask that you continue to align my steps as I search out my purpose through you. Guide my path, Lord, on this journey of life. For I know I was called to greatness through you. Create a new sound mind to see more clearly and increase my faith in you.
In Jesus Name, Amen!

DAY 7: FAITH IN MOTION

Romans 10:17 KJV "So then faith cometh by hearing, and hearing by the word of God."
Acts 3:16 KJV "And his name through faith in his name hath made this man strong, whom ye see and know: yea, the faith which is by him hath given him this perfect soundness in the presence of you all."
Hebrews 11:1 KJV "Now faith is the substance of things hoped for, the evidence of things not seen."
James 2:26 KJV "For as the body without the spirit is dead, so faith without works is dead also."

Faith in motion consists of these three factors:
Speaking Life
What are you saying? Be careful about what you say.
Are you expressing beliefs that contradict what you have faith in regarding God?
Daily affirmations can be beneficial if they are positive.

Hearing the word
Are you actually reading the words, or just listening to everyone else's opinions?
Don't let others' plans distract you.

Taking Action
At some point you have to put some things into action.
The man at the pool of Bethsaida, He kept showing up.
What happens after you have followed all three steps? Are you still willing to show up and ATTEMPT knowing you don't have much of a chance?

Here is an example:
If you are looking for a new car.
Through Speaking Life - Daily Affirmation - I shall have a new car, which won't break me financially.
By Hearing the Word - Romans 4:17 (As it is written, I have made thee a father of many nations,) before him whom he believed, even God, who quickeneth the dead, and calleth those things which be not as though they were.
Taking Action - Save, Browse options, Negotiate the price.
Now I would like to see you put it in action. Write out your 3-step plan.

Prayer
Oh Father God in Heaven, I trust your word in spirit and in truth. I ask that you increase my faith in this walk. Deliver me from the spirit of fear, for I know that faith without works is dead. You are my source of strength in times of weakness. Help me to be more intentional, disciplined, and diligent in this walk. Increase me Lord in all hidden areas of my life. Increase my faith in you. Thank you for mercy and saving me.
In Jesus Name, Amen!

DAY 8: NO LONGER BEING PASSIVE BUT PURPOSEFUL

Colossians 3:23-24 KJV: "And whatsoever ye do, do it heartily, as to the Lord, and not unto men; Knowing that of the Lord ye shall receive the reward of the inheritance: for ye serve the Lord Christ."

If we are honest, there are many moments in our lives when we run on autopilot. In many ways, autopilot is a great thing. It allows us to rest from one task and shift our focus to others. Pilots don't use autopilot during turbulence. The reason is that while a plane can fly in clear skies, there are some factors it cannot detect to stabilize. There are times in our lives when being on auto-pilot is not only inadequate but also risky. We need to shift from passivity to being purposeful during certain seasons of our lives. A pilot can walk through the cabin, talk to passengers, and even check on the flight attendants while on autopilot. There are moments when it's essential to eliminate distractions and concentrate on reaching the destination, which requires your attention. Let's face it: intention demands attention!

If we reach specific destinations, we must take the wheel! This means you can't be passive; you have to be aggressively purposeful. We can't just assume that things will happen; instead, we should come with the mindset that it won't happen unless I turn off the autopilot and take control.

Prayer

Oh, Father God in Heaven, I have been running on autopilot. I ask that you renew my mindset and boost my spirit. Light a fire under me, Lord, so that I may find joy

in serving you wholeheartedly and in my purpose. Release me from this idle and stagnant spirit.
In Jesus Name, Amen!

DAY 9: TRUSTING GOD WHILE BEING YOU

1 Samuel 17:38 KJV: "And Saul armed David with his armour, and he put an helmet of brass upon his head; also he armed him with a coat of mail."
1 Samuel 17:39 KJV: "And David girded his sword upon his armour, and he assayed to go; for he had not proved it. And David said unto Saul, I cannot go with these; for I have not proved them. And David put them off him."

David was the smallest of his brothers, and many didn't believe he belonged near a battle, let alone in one. He wasn't even there to fight; he was tending to the sheep and had to bring something.

David is trying to understand why everyone is so afraid of this Philistine.

Why was David not afraid? He knew whom he served. He had already killed a bear and a lion; who was this man? Once he convinced them to let him fight, Saul began loading him up with armor. Why? The armor served as protection. Everyone used it, but David wasn't built for it. So, this protection had now become a barrier.

How often has someone tried to approach you, but you perceived it as phony because they weren't being themselves? How often were you heading toward your purpose, but someone tried to make you go like them??

Sometimes we can't move forward because we're still trying to do things like everyone else. I understand you want to respect and honor others, but the best way to do that is by being yourself. It's not about what you wear but who you represent. David was serious about his God and his mission. You can succeed and reach your goals, but you must do it your way. It's

okay to admire others, but it's never okay to imitate. If David had acted like everyone else, I believe he wouldn't have survived.
Don't sacrifice yourself by trying to be like someone else.

Prayer
Oh Father God in Heaven, I pray for the spirit of David the warrior. Help me learn to love myself and not compare myself to others. Increase my self-confidence, self-love, and self-care. Lord, help me trust You while being who You have called me to be.
In Jesus Name, Amen!

DAY 10: YOUR ROLE IN GOD'S PLAN

Psalm 37:23 KJV: "The steps of a good man are ordered by the LORD: and he delighteth in his way."

There have been many times in my life when I have contemplated my role in God's great plan. If we're being honest, there are moments when I've tried to discern whether I am operating according to God's will. This isn't meant as a criticism or even a suggestion that I haven't been close enough to God. Have you ever come out of an extended fast or a period of concentration, feeling ready to conquer the world after your time with God, only to be faced with challenges? After Jesus emerged from the wilderness, who was waiting there? Folks used to say it was that old slew-foot devil. Okay, maybe I've aged myself and reveal my country upbringing.

A great way to know if you are truly operating in God's plan is if the devil shows up. How do you know that he appears? It's not when you have minor issues. Minor issues can arise from poor planning, lack of organization, and our shortcomings. When the devil appears, he comes to steal, kill, and destroy. He doesn't want to disrupt your plan; he wants to eliminate God's plan! He's coming to eradicate everything that God has intended. He seeks to kill the plan, steal your confidence in God, and ultimately sever your connection to God.

While many seek to define our place in God's plan, I urge you to solidify your position. Instead of only focusing on whether you are in the right place, concentrate on being rooted and grounded in Him. Because when you are in His plan, the devil will come, and he will come strong! But if you carry the Word, it is quicker and sharper than any two-edged sword(Hebrews 4:12).

Prayer
Oh Father God in Heaven, continue to order my steps and lead me according to your plan, for I am nothing without you! Open my spiritual eyes to see more clearly and increase my spirit of discernment. Let your will be done over my life as I continue to trust in you. Thank you for your guidance.
In Jesus Name, Amen!

PART 3: A TIME TO PIVOT AND A TIME TO MOVE

"There is nothing wrong with shifting, you just have to do so after you maximize where you are first. If you haven't, I suggest Pivoting."

DAY 11: OVERCOMING FEAR

1 Corinthians 15:58 KJV: "Therefore, my beloved brethren, be ye stedfast, unmoveable, always abounding in the work of the Lord, forasmuch as ye know that your labour is not in vain in the Lord."

Many of us are gripped by the fear of loss during this season of closed doors. I know that God has not given us the spirit of fear. So, if you are fearful, it must be coming from somewhere else. Unfortunately, that fear has us scrambling for whatever we need to stay relevant and sustained. As a result, we have begun to act too early and hastily, not trusting in God because of that spirit of fear.

In the story of Daniel in the lion's den, he continued to pray to God despite a new law prohibiting it. He was unafraid because of his trust in God. When thrown into a den of lions, God protected him, and the lions did not harm him. This illustrates how Daniel's faith in God enabled him to remain brave and safe. His faith and fearlessness showcased his confidence in God's ability to protect him, even in the most dangerous situations. Overcoming faith has little to do with what can make you fearful and more to do with the God in whom your trust is in!

Prayer
Oh Father God in Heaven, my labor is not in vain. Grant me the spirit of Daniel. Help me overcome my negative thoughts. Deliver me from the spirit of fear and increase my faith in You. I am capable! Anything is possible

through You, Lord! Continue to uplift me and tear down my imaginations of defeat.
In Jesus Name, Amen!

DAY 12: KNOWING WHEN IT IS TIME TO SHIFT

Ecclesiastes 3:1 KJV: "To everything there is a season, and a time to every purpose under the heaven."

Instead of pivoting, sometimes we should be shifting. There's nothing wrong with shifting; you just have to do it after maximizing your current situation first.

In a car, you go from 1st to 2nd gear to increase speed. The problem is that you won't achieve maximum acceleration if you shift too early. So, how do you know when it's time to shift? When the car stops losing acceleration.

The same principle applies to life. Shifting is necessary once you've reached your maximum capacity in an area; it's time to shift. Pivoting, on the other hand, means doing something completely different. Shifting simply means moving to the next gear.

Perhaps you need a bit more. Consider working in a different department instead of getting upset and quitting your job. Instead of leaving that church, maybe it's time to sit down with the Pastor and explore if there's another ministry where you can serve.

Recognizing when and where to shift is crucial, so pay attention to your surroundings and seek guidance from God.

Prayer

Oh Father God in Heaven, guide me during these uncertain times. Open my eyes to clarity about the direction of my life. Strengthen me to accept when it is time to shift so I can make those changes. Show me when it's time to move on from situations, circumstances,

friendships, careers, or business ventures. Help me avoid one-sided thinking. Help me recognize when it's time to move on so I can advance in my life.
In Jesus Name, Amen!

DAY 13: THE COURAGE TO PIVOT

Jeremiah 6:16 KJV: "Thus saith the LORD, Stand ye in the ways, and see, and ask for the old paths, where is the good way, and walk therein, and ye shall find rest for your souls."

Now that you have shifted and achieved all that you can, it's time to consider a pivot. Pivoting means keeping the same stance but changing direction for a better perspective. The purpose of the pivot is to ensure that you don't lose your position in life or, better yet, your purpose on this earth.

I'm a huge basketball fan and I even do some volunteer coaching. We teach our kids the basics, and part of that is to maintain your pivot foot when you stop dribbling. You can't move forward after you stop dribbling, but you can pivot on one foot to make a play. On that foot, you can pivot and pass or take a shot, but you can't move forward from your previous motion.

Let's take this to church. Many churches have now incorporated various styles into every aspect of their services, whether it's the attire, music selection, dimly lit rooms, or even adding coffee shops. Pivoting can occur while still being "in the game."

You can transition from suits and dresses to jeans and t-shirts, as long as you remember that the Blood of Jesus still covers you.

You can transition from traditional Gospel to contemporary Christian music, as long as you continue to sing about the goodness of God.

See, pivoting means making drastic changes to your approach. As long as you keep the main thing the main thing, everything will work out. I changed jobs and industries once because it no longer allowed me to serve the community I am called to serve. That was a pivot because I could no longer shift where I was.

Next time you are at a crossroad, ask yourself if there is anything else that will allow you to still fulfill your purpose.

Prayer
Oh Father God in Heaven, grant me the courage to pivot when the time is right. Increase my drive, motivation, confidence, and faith! Continue to guide my decision-making skills and lead me along the path you have ordained for me.
In Jesus Name, Amen!

DAY 14: SEEKING GOD'S GUIDANCE IN UNCERTAINTY

Proverbs 4:25 KJV: "Let thine eyes look right on, and let thine eyelids look straight before thee."
Proverbs 4:26 KJV: "Ponder the path of thy feet, and let all thy ways be established."
Proverbs 4:27 KJV: "Turn not to the right hand nor to the left: remove thy foot from evil."

There have been many seasons in my life when I didn't know what to do next. Even though I was unsure, I believe the most challenging thing to endure was knowing whether God would be pleased with my next choice. I know many of us genuinely feel that we must hold on to The Voice and wait to hear from Him. But what if you're in a season where you can't even do that? I've been there, and some of you may have been there as well.

I want to encourage you not to lose hope or faith that God will honor what you do, even during this season. If we acknowledge Him in all our ways, He will direct our paths. My pastor often reminds me that, "as long as you have prayed and acknowledged God, you have put the ball back in His court."

So, what should you do in times of uncertainty? First, seek God and acknowledge Him. After doing that, remember that it's important to keep seeking God and acknowledging Him rather than remaining idle. Moving forward confidently is essential, knowing that even if you make a wrong step, God will guide you back to the right path. I encourage you to stay focused on your mission, your goals, and ultimately on God's calling for your life. Maintain your focus, but always ensure you put God first in everything you do. Once you prioritize Him, acknowledge Him, and seek His guidance, don't forget to take action. Many of us pray repeatedly but never actually follow through with our deeds. If you believe that God will act, the Bible teaches us that faith without works is dead. So yes, believe in God, trust God, and after seeking His guidance and acknowledging Him, it's still crucial to take action.

Prayer
Oh Father God in Heaven, I ask that you lift me up and strengthen me during these times of self-doubt and uncertainty. I acknowledge that you are with me and will never leave or forsake me. I invite you to guide me. Direct my path and let your will be done in my life.
In Jesus Name, Amen!

DAY 15: SEEKING STRENGTH DURING TRANSITION

Proverbs 16:3 KJV: "Commit thy works unto the LORD, and thy thoughts shall be established."

Jesus ends the Last Supper with those who have followed him. He connects with those nearest to him. On this evening, he also gives a warning that even though you're close and have witnessed what I've done, I am about to be denied and betrayed, not by an insider, but by one of you. He would be betrayed and denied by someone in his inner circle. Before Jesus went to the cross in his most vulnerable state, he looked at his twelve disciples and narrowed it down to three. He took them with him to the garden and gave specific instructions on how to wait there and pray.

Jesus expressed his feelings throughout the day and even now. So why didn't they stay awake? Just because Peter, James, and John fell asleep doesn't diminish the pain. The sorrow brought him to his knees. If what you're going through isn't enough, the loneliness can leave you in tears.

Have you ever felt alone in a crowded place?
In this very space, Jesus seeks strength from his friends, focusing on the one who will never leave or forsake us. Jesus exemplifies that when we've relied on others for strength, the best place to find it is with our Father.

Prayer

Oh Father God in Heaven, I dedicate myself to you during this transition in my life. I recognize that my strength comes from you. Please continue to empower me and guide me. For in you alone do I place all my trust.

In Jesus Name, Amen!

PART 4: BE INTENTIONAL WITH BEING THERE FOR YOUR LOVED ONES, FRIENDS, COLLEAGUES.

"And the LORD restored Job's fortunes when he prayed for his friends. And the LORD gave Job twice as much as he had before."

DAY 16: SHOW UP FOR THOSE WE CARE ABOUT

Job 2:13 KJV: "So they sat down with him upon the ground seven days and seven nights, and none spake a word unto him: for they saw that his grief was very great." Galatians 6:2 KJV: "Bear ye one another's burdens, and so fulfill the law of Christ."

Now let's get to the story of Job, a man who had everything many of us could only dream of but lost it all. Even when he lost everything, he had friends. Those three friends came and sat with him, but here's the kicker: they didn't believe that Job had merely experienced a loss. They held their own internal feelings and opinions about why Job lost everything. Some thought he lost everything due to sin or some other reason, but the fact is, they showed up.

So, what's the lesson?
Sometimes your presence is more valuable than your words. Yes, eventually the same friends that showed up for Job had a lot to say but their first act was to say nothing. Over the last few years my family has been very intentional about living the saying of Love Shows Up! My ask of you is to show up for someone that you love. Whether it's a birthday, graduation, or just because - be intentional enough to just show up.

Prayer
Oh Father God in Heaven, your humble servant comes before You to pray for all my loved ones. I pray for a hedge of protection around them. I ask that You guide their minds and hearts back to You, heal them, and strengthen them through whatever trials and tribulations

they may be facing. I pray that You continue to use me as a light and a reflection of Your grace.
In Jesus Name, Amen!

DAY 17: THE GIFT OF BEING PRESENT

1 Peter 4:8 KJV: "And above all things have fervent charity among yourselves: for charity shall cover the multitude of sins."

How we feel about our friend's circumstances—whether we believe they may have cheated the wrong person or caused the pain they are experiencing—should not matter.

They shouldn't have walked off their job. They cursed out their manager; whatever they did doesn't matter in this moment. However, what does matter is your availability and presence. So, our intentional moment for today is to show up for our friends, regardless of our feelings about their situation.

If they are truly your friend, be intentional enough to say, "I may not agree with you, but I'm going to be present with you. I'm going to give you what you need in this moment. We will deal with what happens later. I may be a truth-teller later; we may get down to it and express how I feel. But at this moment, in your immediate loss, I'm going to be intentional about showing up because my presence means something."

When was the last time someone showed up for you?
How did it make you feel?

For me, it has this warm feeling of acceptance. Giving the gift of being present is always about how you make the next person feel. I encourage you to inconvenience yourself to give to others. See, the most precious gift is one that cost you something, whether it is time, money, resources - let your gift be valuable.

Prayer
Oh Father God in Heaven, thank you for allowing me to be present in the lives of my friends and loved ones. Please continue to help me let my light shine and do your will. Assist me in being intentional when it matters and in listening without condemning. Increase my spirit with humility and charity so I can be present when needed. In Jesus Name, Amen!

DAY 18: INTENTIONAL PRAYERS FOR YOUR LOVED ONES

James 5:14 KJV: "Is any sick among you? let him call for the elders of the church; and let them pray over him, anointing him with oil in the name of the Lord:
James 5:15 KJV: "And the prayer of faith shall save the sick, and the Lord shall raise him up; and if he have committed sins, they shall be forgiven him."
James 5:16 KJV: "Confess your faults one to another, and pray one for another, that ye may be healed. The effectual fervent prayer of a righteous man availeth much."

Let's examine Job's three friends: Eliphaz, Bided, and Zophar. As soon as Job began to lose everything, his friends came to console him. This is what we want from our friends. However, the chips quickly turned.

From Chapter 4-23 we see a discussion between Job and his three friends. They begin to talk about what they think happened, but to his face. Job, you must have sinned. God doesn't punish those whom he loves. Eliphaz bodly tells him, "there is no end to your iniquities."

They think they are defending God by pushing all the blame on Job. They believe this because they have usually seen God deal justly. Job maintains his innocence. Yes, he lost everything but still innocent. The Lord then speaks to the Eliphaz in Job 42:7.

After the LORD had spoken these words to Job, the LORD said to Eliphaz the Temanite: "My anger burns against you and your two friends, for you have not spoken of me what is right, as my servant Job has.

They were wrong because they said God was punishing Job when God wasn't. It's okay that people come against you, so let them. Take care of what you need to do, and God will handle the rest. What's interesting though is that the same one they talked about had to pray for them.

God told them, "And my servant Job shall pray for you, for I will accept his prayer not to deal with you according to your folly." Job 42:10

And the LORD restored Job's fortunes when he prayed for his friends. And the LORD gave Job twice as much as he had before.

Are you willing to pray for your friends despite their unjustly behavior towards you?

Prayer
Oh Father God in Heaven, I pray for the covering over my loved ones. I pray for the healing and restoration of them mentally, spiritually, physically, emotionally. I ask that you guide their steps and deliver them from the wiles of the devil.
In Jesus Name, Amen!

DAY 19: SPEAKING LIFE INTO YOUR LOVED ONES

Proverbs 17:17 KJV: "A friend loveth at all times, and a brother is born for adversity."

Sometimes just hearing a " I see you" is the most powerful thing you can listen to. I was working very hard at something, and through the many pitfalls, God was still kind, and things began coming together. While I was stressed about how things were, if things would go together, and if anyone would recognize my efforts. "I See You" was the most amazing feeling. It literally brought me to tears.

We need to find ways to inspire our loved ones. You never know what they might be going through and encouraging them can really brighten their day. Life can be tough sometimes, and we often face it alone. When you are going through it by yourself, it can feel unbearable. This world is complex; let's face it, we need each other. We can't do this alone.

I have a mission for you. Take the next 24 hours and speak life into someone. Be intentional about letting someone know they are not alone and that someone sees them in the middle of their trauma, mess, and all they are going through. See how far an "I See You" will go.

Prayer
Oh Father God in Heaven, please strengthen my faith in You so I can serve my loved ones with righteousness. Deliver me from a negative mindset and restore positive thoughts within me. Continue to help me overcome my

dark moments so that I may be a light and bring life to uplift and encourage others.
In Jesus Name, Amen!

DAY 20: BEING INTENTIONAL WITH CREATING LASTING MEMORIES

Ephesians 4:2 KJV: "With all lowliness and meekness, with longsuffering, forbearing one another in love;" Ephesians 4:3 KJV: "Endeavouring to keep the unity of the Spirit in the bond of peace."

Back when we lived in South Carolina, I owned an insurance agency. When I was in college, one of my career goals was not just to be an entrepreneur but to own my very own insurance agency. Very early in my marriage and my career, before I even turned 25, I was blessed with the opportunity to actually own my own agency. I saw that as a blessing, an accomplishment, and something truly amazing. However, what I realized is that as time went on, around the second year, it began to pull me away from my family.

You have to understand how I was raised. I was taught that a man should provide. At that time, I wasn't just providing; I was providing very well, even more than I could have imagined. However, I had a lot to learn quickly, and what I needed to know had little to do with money and more to do with time. I was going through a transition at the office and was deeply immersed in my work. I would work all day at the business, and then at night, whether at the office or home, I had to continue working on it, which left me with little to no time for my family. The breaking point came one evening when it was pitch black outside, and I could see the entryway from my office. I saw my wife bringing our son and daughter, who was in a car seat because she was still an infant, to my office just to check on me. In that moment, I realized that I was missing out on time and memories.

I encourage you not to miss out on memories by chasing only temporary things. We live in a time when many people are so busy trying to absorb and capture what they see instead of living in the moments they are experiencing. What do I mean? Have you ever been at a conference? Have you ever been at a concert? Have you ever been in church and seen everyone with their phones out trying to capture the moment?

I want to encourage you to avoid missing out on moments and be very intentional about how you live in those moments. Don't spend too much time trying to capture a moment that you can rewind and see later on a device. Truth be told, if you lose that device, you also lose that memory. However, what you can never lose is the feeling that a memory creates when you are intentional about being present in the moment. So, be intentional about being present in your family life during the moments you create together and in the time, you spend with your loved ones.

Prayer

Oh Father God in Heaven, thank you for all my blessings. I am grateful for the people in my life, and I ask that you continue to place like-minded spirits in my path. Increase my zeal for family and spending time with loved ones, for I know that tomorrow isn't promised.
In Jesus Name, Amen!

PART 5: BE INTENTIONAL WITH YOUR FAITH WALK

"It's not just what you believe but how your actions show what you have faith in."

DAY 21: FAITH IN UNCERTAINTY

Hebrews 11:1 KJV: "Now faith is the substance of things hoped for, the evidence of things not seen."
Hebrews 11:3 KJV: "Through faith we understand that the worlds were framed by the word of God, so that things which are seen were not made of things which do appear."

Faith without works is dead, yes. But just because you work doesn't mean you will immediately see results either. Faith is such a complex concept. It requires us to invest effort in something we can't currently perceive, while potentially not reaping the benefits later. Imagine working at an assembly plant for a car. Your job is to wrap the steering wheel with leather. You do an amazing job putting the wheel together. In fact, you are the best in the company at doing it. However, you never see the steering wheel in the actual finished car. You are a master of that piece but not the entire puzzle.

Faith without works doesn't mean you work the entire vision, it means you work what you have been assigned. I talked with my pastor and he encouraged me, like REALLY! I spoke to him about where I am in ministry and whether now is the time for change. Then he just did the unthinkable. He began telling me that the ministry I lead in Florida was of God and possibly not how I thought. He said that His commission and promise was that the Gospel be heard all over the earth. So that when anyone gets to heaven, no one can say they have not heard because he sent a prophet. He told me that for the years we were established as a church, we were fulfilling that, and if things change, God would be pleased because the call on us all is to spread the gospel. I knew that I had done that, but as a church baby, I always saw longevity as success, not purpose. So, I did my small and even tiny piece to God's ultimate vision of ensuring everyone heard the Gospel.

Be faithful and work what you have been assigned. Even if you can't see your steering wheel on the showroom floor, God is pleased.

Prayer
Oh Father God in Heaven, strengthen my faith and replace my fears with trust. Deliver me from anxiety and insecurity. Enhance my wisdom in your word and renew my mind and spirit as I strive to accomplish everything I set out to achieve.
In Jesus Name, Amen!

DAY 22: YOU REAP WHAT YOU SOW

Matthew 25:26 KJV: "His lord answered and said unto him, Thou wicked and slothful servant, thou knewest that I reap where I sowed not, and gather where I have not strawed:
Matthew 25:27 "Thou oughtest therefore to have put my money to the exchangers, and then at my coming I should have received mine own with usury."
1 Corinthians 3:8 KJV: "Now he that planteth and he that watereth are one: and every man shall receive his own reward according to his own labour."

One thing I have come to understand as a business owner is that we should not invest our time and resources into opportunities that will not yield results. I have a friend who is a financial advisor and professor; he teaches people how to invest in the stock market. I have also spent nearly 20 years working in the financial industry in various roles.

I've learned that great investments may not always align with your personal preferences. There will be times when they might clash, but they can still be good investments—absolutely! I'm a fan of sneakers, especially Jordans. I once told a colleague I would be a sneakerhead, but my wife won't let me. Let's face it, shoes are expensive. Investing in Nike is a natural move because of my attraction to their products. Millions of others feel the same way, and due to its popularity and business model, Nike is definitely worth considering as an investment. If you had invested 20 years ago, it would have paid off tremendously today, growing over 800%. However, you must also understand the economics behind Nike and why it was such a great investment—not just because many people like their shoes, or even because you personally do, but because it was a solid business idea with a well-structured plan.

The next time you are sowing into something, weigh whether it is a heart move or is it strategic to where you are going. Be intentional about where you sow!

Prayer
Oh Father God in Heaven, cleanse me of my iniquities and open my eyes to my mistakes. Lord, help me overcome my faults and make better, righteous decisions. Deliver me from a slothful spirit and a spirit of fear. I understand that if I don't sow the seed, it won't reap. Guide my path to sow my seeds wisely and appropriately.
In Jesus Name, Amen!

DAY 23: UNDERSTANDING TRUE INVESTMENTS

Ecclesiastes 11:6 KJV: "In the morning sow thy seed, and in the evening withhold not thine hand: for thou knowest not whether shall prosper, either this or that, or whether they both shall be alike good."
1 Corinthians 16:2 KJV: "Upon the first day of the week let every one of you lay by him in store, as God hath prospered him, that there be no gatherings when I come."

Successful investments aren't coincidental; they arise from a purposeful process of identifying, investigating, and pursuing opportunities that resonate with our objectives. To enhance this consideration, reflect on how you invest your most cherished resources. In this regard, two of our greatest assets are money and time.
The teachings of the Bible resonate profoundly here, particularly in Matthew 6:21 (KJV), which states, "For where your treasure is, there your heart will be also." This passage encourages us to examine our priorities and the decisions we make regarding our resources.

Ask yourself these crucial questions:
Where do you choose to place your treasure?
Are your investments directed toward areas that promote personal and professional growth, or are they scattered without intention?

When you intentionally invest your time and money in spaces that foster development and enrichment, you cultivate a harvest reflective of that intent. By aligning your resources with growth-oriented opportunities, you set the stage for meaningful rewards in the future. Evaluate your choices carefully, as they will ultimately shape the direction of your life and the fulfillment of your aspirations.

Prayer
Oh Father God in Heaven, I ask that you open new doors and opportunities. I pray for growth and success over my seeds of investments. Please don't let them be in vain, Lord. Bless me so that I may be a blessing to others. Help me to make investments that will benefit me and my family spiritually, mentally, and financially.
In Jesus Name, Amen!

DAY 24: INTENTIONAL IN EVERYDAY DECISIONS

Ephesians 2:10 KJV: "For we are his workmanship, created in Christ Jesus unto good works, which God hath before ordained that we should walk in them."

Some days I just want to let life be what it is. I don't want to make any decisions and just let whatever happens, happen. Well, there is nothing wrong with having one of those days. The issue arises when you live with an abundance of those days. See, there is a difference between just taking a break and breaking down. Many of the problems we face with becoming intentional about everyday decisions stem from our distaste for being micromanaged. Let's face it, no one likes to be micromanaged, so why do we do that to ourselves? The constant feeling of someone watching your every move, wondering when you will ever be finished or ready to move on to the next thing.

What if I told you that you can manage yourself without the emotions that come with it?

Here it is: create a plan, schedule, and then tackle it. Within that plan, designate a moment (however long it may be) and call it "given grace." You are giving yourself grace not to think or even act. Everyone needs rest and a break from it all. Doing so gives you the time to return and tackle everything you need to accomplish.

As a manager, I am adamant about ensuring my team takes their breaks. Sometimes they might get tired of hearing it from me, but it's for their own good. Yes, it helps keep us compliant but maximizes their productivity. Without moments to relax their minds, burnout can happen quickly. So as you plan your day, be intentional about scheduling breaks, but also be proactive in taking those breaks yourself.

Many things in our lives don't happen because they just dropped out of the sky. Those who are successful will tell you that they worked hard to get to where they are. Whether it's an athlete or a business person, they've had to make certain sacrifices to ensure that success is possible and achieved. God didn't create us to be mediocre; therefore, we shouldn't be satisfied with just getting by but should work diligently to become something that the Father would be proud of.

Prayer

Oh Father God in Heaven, thank you for this day. I choose to be intentional in my decision-making today and every day moving forward. Help me, Lord, to be purposeful in my relationships and time, and to remain in the spirit of Christ. Increase my wisdom and discernment. Guide my mind and thoughts so that I can live with purpose and intention.
In Jesus Name, Amen!

DAY 25: GOD'S FAITHFULNESS

Matthew 6:33 KJV: "But seek ye first the kingdom of God, and his righteousness; and all these things shall be added unto you."
Matthew 7:7 KJV: "Ask, and it shall be given you; seek, and ye shall find; knock, and it shall be opened unto you."

If we are honest with ourselves, trusting God is not an easy task. There have been times when I wondered if God was paying attention. Like, do you see me drowning? Am I really his child, and if so, why would he let me go through this? Maybe you have felt that way, possibly even feel that way now. Well, God sees and hears you and will deliver you.

He Sees You

- The first thing he sees is you.
- You normally can sense someone watching you. You have that eerie feeling that makes you look around. The thing about it is, you have to be close enough to the person in order to get that feeling. God wants you to feel that He has His eyes on you. So just know that the reason you can feel him is because he is close to you.

He Hears You

- It's the righteous who cry, and he hears them. So, it's okay to cry. If there is one thing that we know, parents can't bear to see their children cry. It's something that pulls and tugs at your heartstrings.
- Sometimes we are crying due to our many afflictions.

- o We experience afflictions like any other person, such as illness, finances, and so on.

- o We also experience affliction due to the work we do for Christ. Scripture tells us that many are the afflictions of the righteous.

The reason he sees you and hears you is that he is drawn to your broken heart. This is reminded in Psalms 34:18, which states that he is near to those with a broken heart. I am grateful to serve a God who won't let my heart cry out without action. He delivers! David said, "The righteous cry, and the Lord hears and delivers them out of all their troubles." After he sees your broken heart and hears it, he then delivers you from that pain!

Our God is so faithful that he will never go back on his word.

Prayer
Oh Father God in Heaven, I praise and honor your name. Thank you for your faithfulness in my life and for never leaving my side. Forgive me for the times I have failed to trust in You. Please continue to strengthen my faith so I can remain devoted on this righteous path of serving You.
In Jesus Name, Amen!

PART 6: THERE IS POWER IN BEING PURPOSEFUL, SHOW UP ON PURPOSE

"Doing what you love drives you, while doing what you're called to do represents your purpose; however, the motor behind both is your intentions."

DAY 26: BUILDING TRUST IN YOUR JOURNEY

Hebrews 12:1 KJV: "Wherefore seeing we also are compassed about with so great a cloud of witnesses, let us lay aside every weight, and the sin which doth so easily beset us,"
Hebrews 12:2 KJV: "Looking unto Jesus the author and finisher of our faith; who for the joy that was set before him endured the cross, despising the shame, and is set down at the right hand of the throne of God."

We find here the disciples who are with Jesus, looking and expecting him to do something. You gotta do something! You're down here sleeping while the storm is about to take us out.

I find it concerning, especially since some of these disciples were fishermen by trade. So, you mean to tell me that there's water you haven't seen before and these conditions in the sea are unfamiliar? This can't be the worst sea you've ever encountered. I can't believe that. It's hard for me to accept that, as fishermen and businessmen, they think this is the worst storm they've ever seen. But because Jesus was on board, I believe they felt there was no need for them to think with the abilities he had given them. They felt there was no reason to feel safe just because he's on board; they needed him to do something about it. It's not that we are safe because he's on board; we need him to address the wind, the water, and the fact that we're in this predicament.

But when Jesus performed what he did, he spoke to the wind and the sea, and they were amazed not because they were safe. They were amazed because of the wind and the sea, or because

they obeyed his voice. They were not surprised since they were now okay. They were amazed by how he did it. But Jesus questioned them and asked, "Where's your faith?" Not just faith in him, because their faith in Jesus helped the storm cease, calming the winds and the water, allowing them to be safe. That was their faith in Jesus because they activated it by going to get him. But the faith Jesus asks for is,
"Where is your faith that everything is going to be okay?"

Jesus' ministry was not to die in the sea. He was not going to perish in the ocean; he had to go to Calvary. So, if he has to go to Calvary, that means this ocean can't be the last piece. Everything that you've seen me do, why is that not activated? So, my question is, Jesus is on board. Jesus lives inside of us. He's present. It's time for us to stop being merely intentional with our faith in him and performing miracles, and be more deliberate about activating our faith because he is present; he will not be destroyed.

So, the next time you find yourself in your storm season, when life gets tough, don't ask Him to perform. Don't request that He intervene to stop this person, quiet my manager, or make my children behave; I need a new job. Instead, ask Him this: God, strengthen my faith so that I can make it through the storm, because my faith rests in the fact that You are on board. I don't need to see another miracle to know You're faithful. I don't need to see another miracle to understand that You are a healer. I don't need to see another miracle to recognize that You are a chain breaker. My faith does not hinge on the next miracle; my faith is grounded in knowing that You are with me. So, we are intentional not to ask Him to perform, but we're going to be intentional about sitting and waiting on Him because as long as He's on board, everything will be alright.

<u>Prayer</u>
Oh Father God in Heaven, I trust you on this journey. Yes, I will trust you with every part of who I am. I surrender it all to you. No weapon formed against me shall prosper. You are the Alpha and the Omega. I will stand firm on this journey with your Word at the forefront of my life. All things are possible when we place our trust in you and you alone.
In Jesus Name, Amen!

DAY 27: SETTING SPIRITUAL GOALS

James 1:22 KJV: "But be ye doers of the word, and not hearers only, deceiving your own selves."

Spiritual goals are wonderful to have, but we must be cautious not to set unrealistic objectives. This can go both ways; you can have goals that are either too small or too big for you. Let's first address the goals that are too large. Understand me clearly: I do not mean that anything is too hard for God. However, many of us are attempting to fit stadium-sized goals into storage room vessels. One lesson I've learned is to never push beyond my capacity. If you want to fail quickly, try to occupy a space you can't support. Furnishing a 10,000 square foot home requires far more than what is needed for a 1,000 square foot home. Working with goals that you cannot effectively manage is a recipe for stress, headaches, and frustration.

Some of us tend to set goals that are clearly too small. If God has given you the ability to fill the stadium, it's crucial that you don't limit yourself to the storage room. Jesus even reminds us in Luke 12:48 that to whom much is given, much will be required. If we are honest, many of us operate in smaller spaces to easily achieve success and avoid the stress of doubting our ability to accomplish our goals.

Here is a great recipe for setting spiritual goals:
First understand your capacity.
- Understanding how much you can take physically, emotionally, and spiritually is important.

Identify how your gifts will play a part.
- Setting goals that require you to operate in gifts that you don't possess is a set up for disaster.

- Instead, focus on creating goals that allow you to operate in your gifts.

Determine if your goals are scripturally based and supported.
- You can't have spiritual goals that don't line up with God's word. Psalms 119:105 says Thy word is a lamp unto my feet, and a light unto my path.

Be prepared to be stretched.
- God will stretch you because after all we serve a big God and he's never going to do things that are mediocre.

Acknowledge him.
- It's important that you bring your goals to God. In doing so, you allow him the flexibility to adjust them to align with his will.
- Proverbs 3:6 instructs us to in all thy ways acknowledge him, and he shall direct thy paths.

With all this said, be ready for God to interrupt your goals. Not in a bad way, but in a manner that brings him glory. Are there any goals in your life that you need God to adjust?

Prayer
Oh Father God in Heaven, I seek your guidance in setting my goals. Grant me the wisdom and confidence to align my aspirations with your will for my life. Reveal my potential and strengthen my patience and spirit so I may be diligent. Lord, help me achieve and conquer everything I set out to do if it is within the path You have laid out for me.
In Jesus Name, Amen!

DAY 28: THE CURSE OF PROCRASTINATION

1 Corinthians 9:24 KJV: "Know ye not that they which run in a race run all, but one receiveth the prize? So run, that ye may obtain."

Many students wait until the very last minute to finish their assignments, often hoping for a final chance from their teacher to catch up. However, it's much better to complete work as it is given so that it's turned in on time. Waiting until the last moment can make it harder to grasp the lessons, which can negatively affect scores on quizzes and tests.

Quizzes and tests are scheduled regardless of when assignments are completed. If students keep up with their work ahead of time, they won't have to rush around at the last minute. By tackling assignments bit by bit each day before they are due, they can better prepare for tests and quizzes through more effective studying. This approach also highlights the importance of being proactive every day, whether in school or on our spiritual journey.

In this walk, procrastination isn't our friend. We have to make sure we are proactive each day with our walk towards Christ and our daily goals.

Prayer
Oh Father God in Heaven, help me overcome my struggles with procrastination and fear. Remove this lazy spirit from me so that I can fulfill all the tasks set before me with confidence. Guide me through it, Lord. Renew my mind with positive thoughts and uplift my energy.
In Jesus Name, Amen!

DAY 29: PRIORITIZING SPIRITUAL GROWTH OVER TEMPORARY PLEASURES

Colossians 1:10 KJV: "That ye might walk worthy of the Lord unto all pleasing, being fruitful in every good work, and increasing in the knowledge of God."

There is a parable in the Bible where a man gives money to different individuals to see what they will do with it. He returns and asks them, "What did you do with my money? Let me take a look at it." One individual gave it back to him, saying, "Hey, I have your money, but I also earned some interest. In other words, I grew your money. I was able to flip it and turn it into more than what you initially gave me." The other simply said, "I put it in a safe place to ensure I returned exactly what I received. I was afraid of losing it, so I was intentional about keeping it safe." Many of us operate in a safety zone!
One of the men was intentional about making sure he gave him more than what he received. The other was focused on ensuring he kept what he had given him. "Master, you gave me 10, so I'll give you 10 back!" Yes, the other one may have given you 20, but there was a chance you would have received nothing. The goal isn't to have the most, and it wasn't to have the least. The point I want to emphasize is their intentions followed their hearts. They both made a significant effort to ensure that what they aimed to see happen at the end actually occurred.

Doing what you love drives you; doing what you're called to do is your purpose, but the motivation behind both is your intentions.

<u>Prayer</u>
Oh Father God in Heaven, increase my spirit in righteousness. I seek your guidance to overcome worldly thoughts and the spirit of covetousness. Enhance my spirit of maturity and discernment so that I can recognize when I am walking in the direction of lust and temporary pleasure. Deliver me from it.
In Jesus Name, Amen!

DAY 30: IDENTIFYING YOUR GIFTS

1 Corinthians 12:4 KJV: "Now there are diversities of gifts, but the same Spirit.
1 Corinthians 12:5 KJV: "And there are differences of administrations, but the same Lord."
1 Corinthians 12:6 KJV: "And there are diversities of operations, but it is the same God which worketh all in all."

Growing up, we played a game called guessing the jellybeans in the jar. You might remember it. You would place what seemed like hundreds of jellybeans in a jar, and people would go around guessing how many beans were inside. The interesting thing about the jar was that, since it was clear, everyone could see the same beans. Each person had their own method of guessing. Some relied on the eye test, others counted layers, and some made good old-fashioned educated guesses. The winner would take home the jar. No matter the method, everyone had a chance to solve the puzzle.

We often treat our gifts like a jar of jellybeans. We look, observe, and even get creative in guessing how to use our gifts based on what we see from the outside. You have to break open the jar and count how many beans are inside. For instance, some people love music, but until you open your mouth, you won't know if you can sing. Some people love reading, but until you put pen to paper, how would you know if you are an author? It's one thing to look through the outside, but it's another to open the jar and put in the effort.

The easiest way to understand your gift is to simply try. You may be gifted in storytelling, but that can take many forms. It can be through film, journalism, music, or writing; the way to discover this is to try. No matter what your gift is, it is a gift from God and will never benefit only you. Your gift does nothing when it sits on a shelf, allowing people to stare and guess what's inside. It's only beneficial when you crack open the jar and share it with others who might only see it from their own shell.

<u>Prayer</u>
Oh Father God in Heaven, thank you for blessing me with many gifts. Please help me to bring forth and share my gifts with others. Open my eyes to identify any hidden gifts I may not be aware of so I can bless others. Forgive me for when I have not shared my gifts with others and help me do better.
In Jesus Name, Amen!

PART 7: YOU INVEST IN WHAT WILL BE FRUITFUL, NOT IN WHAT YOU LOVE

"When you are intentional about placing your treasure in spaces of growth, harvest is what you reap."

DAY 31: BEING PURPOSEFUL

Acts 3:1 KJV: "Acts 3:1 Now Peter and John went up together into the temple at the hour of prayer, being the ninth hour."
Acts 3:2 KJV: "And a certain man lame from his mother's womb was carried, whom they laid daily at the gate of the temple which is called Beautiful, to ask alms of them that entered into the temple; Acts 3:3 Who seeing Peter and John about to go into the temple asked an alms."
Acts 3:4 KJV: "And Peter, fastening his eyes upon him with John, said, Look on us."
Acts 3:5 KJV: "And he gave heed unto them, expecting to receive something of them."
Acts 3:6 KJV: "Then Peter said, Silver and gold have I none; but such as I have give I thee: In the name of Jesus Christ of Nazareth rise up and walk."
Acts 3:7 KJV: "And he took him by the right hand, and lifted him up: and immediately his feet and ankle bones received strength."
Acts 3:8 KJV: "And he leaping up stood, and walked, and entered with them into the temple, walking, and leaping, and praising God."

Every one of us reaches a point where we make a conscious decision about our path, whether in our careers or personal lives. Being intentional signifies our actions are deliberate and purposeful; for example, when I say, "I meant to go to work," it highlights that my presence is not by chance—it's a choice. On the other hand, consistency refers to the habit of repeating those actions regularly. I cannot simply choose to go to work sporadically; if I show up inconsistently, my paycheck will also reflect that inconsistency.

There's an underlying expectation connected to this; I anticipate receiving a specific amount—let's call it "X"—for the work I have completed. This brings us to an essential equation:

So, the formula is: **Intentionality + Consistency = Expectation**

While many individuals maintain a consistent awareness of their desires and expectations, it is crucial to reflect on what you have actively chosen to pursue with intention and steadfastness until those expectations materialize.

So, think about it:

What commitments have you decided to be intentional and consistent in?

What steps are you taking to turn your aspirations into reality?

Prayer

Oh Father God in Heaven, help me to be more purposeful. Purge any impatience that resides within me. Help me to be more diligent in this walk and intentional in everything I aim to do. Continue to lead and guide me on my path of righteousness.
In Jesus Name, Amen!

DAY 32: ALIGNING ACTIONS WITH PURPOSE

Philippians 3:13 KJV: "Brethren, I count not myself to have apprehended: but this one thing I do, forgetting those things which are behind, and reaching forth unto those things which are before,"
Philippians 3:14 KJV: "I press toward the mark for the prize of the high calling of God in Christ Jesus."

People in need are usually found where they think assistance can be provided. If I need food, I'll linger in places where people are eating. If I need money, I'll stay in places where people are spending money. If I need medicine, I'll be around the hospital. If I want a drink, I'll frequent the ABC store.

There is a scripture that references a lame man that was late at the gate of the temple daily. You may be familiar with this passage. The Bible never states that he was poor; it only mentions that he was lame from birth. We often associate begging with poverty. The Bible notes that he was laid out daily to ask for alms. The word "alms" comes from the Greek term "eleemosyne," which means "compassion or pity," and is derived from the word "eleos," meaning "mercy."

What if he wasn't asking for money but for something more???

From the text, I see someone who feels unworthy. He likely believes that he has never been enough since he was born. So he goes to the place he thinks will provide him compassion, mercy, and pity. He goes there intentionally and consistently - but people keep giving him money!

One day you are going to keep showing up but someone is going to bless you with what you need. So, show up even if they have lay you there!

Prayer

Oh Father God in Heaven, grant me clarity and direction that align with my purpose. Help me to see the opportunities you have placed before me. Grant me the courage to advance in faith and succeed according to your will.

In Jesus Name, Amen!

DAY 33: CREATING A PURPOSE-DRIVEN ENVIRONMENT

Psalm 138:8 KJV: "The LORD will perfect that which concerneth me: thy mercy, O LORD, endureth for ever: forsake not the works of thine own hands."

Have you ever felt the frustration of being misunderstood? It's a challenge we often encounter when others perceive our needs or intentions differently than we intended. Imagine a scenario where someone believes you are seeking one specific thing, but in reality, your heart longs for something far deeper and more meaningful.

Consider the encounter between Peter and a man who was crippled from birth. When Peter caught sight of him, he confidently declared, "Look at us." The man turned to them, his eyes filled with hope, perhaps expecting a few coins or some spare change to alleviate his immediate plight. However, what happened next was nothing short of transformative.

Instead of the anticipated gesture of handing over coins, Peter reached deep within himself and offered the man something profoundly more valuable. He didn't simply dismiss the man's gaze or say, "Nah, I'm only looking for money." Instead, he extended his hand, offering hope and healing. In that moment, I can almost hear the man's unspoken thoughts, "This is what I was waiting for!" A moment of revelation shifted the course of his life entirely, illustrating the profound difference between mere survival and true fulfillment.

Prayer

Oh Father God in Heaven, help me create a positive environment. Remove any distractions that hinder me

*from reaching my goals. Align me with like-minded spirits who will help and guide me to achieve my goals. Create a purpose-driven, righteous environment.
In Jesus Name, Amen!*

DAY 34: THE IMPORTANCE OF QUALITY TIME

1 Thessalonians 5:11 KJV: "Wherefore comfort yourselves together, and edify one another, even as also ye do."

There comes a point when we want to win in our darkest moments—when we get sick, when someone passes away, or when emotional pain strikes. Sometimes, all we desire is for someone to be present. In the midst of your sorrow, your closest friends arrive not with words or solutions, but simply to be by your side.

Can you imagine a world where, the next time you lose something, your closest friends come just to visit you—not to say anything, but to simply sit with you?

Picture them settling into the space around you, silent yet supportive, reminding you that you are not alone in your grief. The comfort of shared silence, the warmth of companionship during trying times. There's incredible power in spending meaningful time with friends when they need solace the most. Their presence serves as a gentle reminder of love and understanding, providing comfort to the wounds of pain and heartache.

Prayer
Oh Father God in Heaven, thank you for helping me recognize the importance of family and quality time. Please assist me in enhancing my spirit of empathy and sympathy, so I can cherish every moment spent with my loved ones.

In Jesus Name, Amen!

DAY 35: STAY FOCUSED

Colossians 3:1-2 KJV "If ye then be risen with Christ, seek those things which are above, where Christ sitteth on the right hand of God. Set your affection on things above, not on things on the earth."

With everything happening in the world, it's imperative that we stay focused. An eye doctor advises you to place one hand over your eye. We can achieve instant gratification on our own with minimal assistance from others. Earthly pleasures are not only instant but also provide a sense of self-fulfilling gratification.

Here are some things on the earth that are intriguing to us.
- Cars
- Houses
- Money

You should seek the things that are above, but you also have a connection to what's near.
- Joy
- Meekness
- Kindness
- Relationship with Christ

Things from above require time, resources, and patience. They also reflect the ability to impact others in our effort to have joy, it becomes contagious. Kindness is a reflection of how you treat others. Stay focused on those things every day.

<u>Prayer</u>
Oh Father God in Heaven, thank you for not giving up on me in my weakest moments of self-fulfillment. Deliver me from a worldly, covetous mindset. Increase my spirit of patience and obedience to stay focused on your word. I thank you for your mercy and grace over my life.
In Jesus Name, Amen!

PART 8: BE INTENTIONAL WITH YOUR WALK IN CHRIST

Psalms 116:12 "What shall I render unto the LORD for all his benefits toward me?"

DAY 36: INTENTIONAL LIVING

Luke 8:23 KJV: "But as they sailed he fell asleep: and there came down a storm of wind on the lake; and they were filled with water, and were in jeopardy."
Luke 8:24 KJV: "And they came to him, and awoke him, saying, Master, master, we perish. Then he arose, and rebuked the wind and the raging of the water: and they ceased, and there was a calm."
Luke 8:25 KJV: "And he said unto them, Where is your faith? And they being afraid wondered, saying one to another, What manner of man is this! for he commandeth even the winds and water, and they obey him."

One thing is very true in our house: whenever it's date night for my wife and me, or when we have to be away for an extended period, the kids always find ways to ensure they're fed, entertained, and have what they need. However, since we live in Florida, we often face hurricanes and similar events, school becomes essential as it protects the kids and provides shelters for those needing higher ground by utilizing the schools.

As a result, we spend a lot of unplanned time together. Yet, it amazes me how, whenever my wife and I are around, the kids don't seem to know what to do. They ask for help with meals: What are we cooking? What are we eating for lunch? What are we having for a snack?

Don't get me wrong, my kids can manage on their own; I have a 16-year-old and an 12-year-old now, so they can handle things themselves. They can cook their own breakfast, prepare their own lunches, and do all that, but when their parents are

home, especially if mom is around, they expect her to do something for them.
It's important that we live with intentions everyday without depending on others.

What would you do if it's just you?

<u>Prayer</u>
*Oh Father God in Heaven, help us to live with intentionality. As we go about our day, help us to live each day with meaning and purpose. Even when we are not feeling our best, help us to live each day with an intentional heart. Guide our steps this day so that when we are hesitant we still walk according to your will.
In Jesus Name, Amen!*

DAY 37: DAILY SURRENDER

Psalms 116:12 KJV: "What shall I render unto the LORD for all his benefits toward me?"
1 Corinthians 15:31 KJV: "I protest by your rejoicing which I have in Christ Jesus our Lord, I die daily."

God wants more from you. You haven't given him enough. God needs more. What shall I render? Many of us have been asking God to come into our houses, and now that he's here, he's asking for more. He's not just asking for more; he is also REQUIRING more!
For some of us its....
Time: Some of us have been sleeping too well.
How much time do you spend entertaining yourself?
Have you been on more vacations than days you've fasted?
Resources: Items in the home: clothes, electronics, and more.
Finances
Car: Are you worshipping your car? Will you offer charity and pick someone up for church?

For some of us, it's a bit more intangible. God asks you to show a little more grace. The bottom line is that we've become a little too Comfortable.
Have we forgotten that this world is NOT our home????
You've Got More in You!

Prayer
Oh Father God in Heaven, help us to understand what true surrender is. While we have an idea of what it means, help us to get closer and closer to relinquishing our own

will to surrender to yours. When we stray from your will begin to follow ours, remind us that there is power in surrendering to you.
In Jesus Name, Amen!

DAY 38: CHRIST AT THE CENTER OF YOUR LIFE

John 5:7 KJV: "7. The impotent man answered him, Sir, I have no man, when the water is troubled, to put me into the pool: but while I am coming, another steppeth down before me."
John 5:8 KJV: "Jesus saith unto him, Rise, take up thy bed, and walk."
John 5:9 KJV: "And immediately the man was made whole, and took up his bed, and walked: and on the same day was the sabbath."

Never stop showing up. In Jerusalem, there was a poll near the sheep market. What was amazing about it is that an angel would come and stir the water during a certain season. Whoever went in first would be healed of whatever disease they had. Here we find a man who had been infirm for 38 years. He had been coming to the pool, but no one was there to put him in. Now, if people had to carry you there, what makes you think you could get into the pool before those who could move?

Maybe he thought, "These people are sick too, so I might have a chance." The truth is, we all know someone who, if given the chance... would take your spot. Even if they didn't need it as badly as you.

What would you have done if you couldn't beat everyone around you?
- Would you have given up?
- Would you even show up?

This man not only showed up but also made an attempt on his own!

Are you still willing to show up and attempt, knowing you don't have much of a chance?

Prayer

Oh Father God in Heaven, When life gets tough and friends get few help us to keep you at the center. While we plan and attack, help us to remember that we do it all for you. Every attempt is meant to please you and we asked that when you are not pleased, teach us to make you happy. You are the center of joy and our life.

In Jesus Name, Amen!

DAY 39: FINDING INTENTIONAL JOY IN TODAY

Psalms 32:11 KJV: "Be glad in the LORD, and rejoice, ye righteous: and shout for joy, all ye that are upright in heart."

I was out of town and decided to go into the mall to pick up a few things. While I was there, a man approached me. Now, anyone who's ever been in a mall knows that the salespeople at the kiosks in the middle aren't afraid to approach you. I thought this was just another sales pitch, but I smiled and greeted him as he came closer. As he walked up, he raised his fist, and I thought, what is this? Of course, I'm out of town, but a raised fist can't be good. Yet he was smiling—was this good or bad? Well, he approached and wanted a fist bump. I thought, okay, we're in the clear—no violence today. He said with a smile, "I just want you to know that Jesus loves you." Wow! The person in me felt amazing that someone approached me with such kind words. The Christian in me was grateful for the reminder and felt joy. Now the minister in me became intrigued. I was intrigued because he didn't hand me any material about God's Plan for my life. He didn't seek conversation. He simply said what he said and kept walking. Then I noticed him fist bumping other people in the mall, and the minister in me woke up. See, it's not always about how many people you can get to come to your church; it's not always about giving them material on preparing for His return. Sometimes, it's just good to let people know that Jesus loves them with no agenda. I'm grateful for this man who intentionally spread joy in a mall on a random Saturday. He had no shopping bags, no fancy suit, or even Jesus merch. Just a smile, a fist bump, and words meant to intentionally inspire people through Christ.

Prayer
Oh Father God in Heaven, Teach us to count it all joy when we fall into temptation. Teach us to count it all joy when our plans don't go the way we would have them too. Teach us to count it all joy when others stray. We ask these things because our joy comes from you.
In Jesus Name, Amen!

DAY 40: TRUSTING GOD TO LEAD IN NEW DIRECTIONS

Isaiah 43:18-19 KJV: "Remember ye not the former things, neither consider the things of old. Behold, I will do a new thing; now it shall spring forth; shall ye not know it? I will even make a way in the wilderness, and rivers in the desert."

Have you ever been in such a difficult situation that you felt nervous about how you would make it out? Maybe you are in that situation right now. Even though you have seen God perform healings, miracles, signs, and wonders, there may still be some doubt that he will bring you out of this particular circumstance. Why? It's mainly because, despite all that he has done before, this feels different. I've learned that the Devil is very cunning; he knows us and studies us. When he attacks, he is strategic and never strikes without hitting us where it hurts. Sometimes we need a reminder of exactly who God is. The fact remains that he will never leave us or forsake us. In protecting his people, sometimes he has to do something new—something we have never seen before. However, we can't be stuck in the ways of old. We can't limit God in how he is going to bring us out.

Let's make it practical. Perhaps the last time you faced financial troubles, you received an unexpected check. What if this time, God is going to bless you with another source of income? Some of us might be skeptical about this new source of income because we are focused on God sending us a check.

We must take the time to expect not only something greater but also something different from God. To receive what God has in store for us, we need to be open to what he is going to do.

Prayer
Oh Father God in Heaven, Help us to trust you in not only the good times but also the bad times. Help us to know that you will never leave us or forsake us. Even when we have planned, strategized, and put our faith in motion - help us to trust that you will lead and guide us. As we move intentionally through life, we ask that you continue to send Grace and Mercy to follow us. We will make mistakes and we will fall but knowing that you are near will make the difference. Thank you for not only being The God that hears but also The God that understands!
In Jesus Name, Amen!

ACKNOWLEDGMENTS

Without those who pushed me to be great and inspired me to put pen to paper on what God gave me, this wouldn't be possible. I want to say thank you. To everyone who has ever said that I inspire them to be great, thank you. This book would not be possible if I couldn't draw on the appreciation felt from your words of kindness and encouragement. To all my Emmanuel family, know that I love you and that many of your prayers for me and my family have contributed to where I am today. To my amazing pastor, Bishop Rickie Jackson, who continuously sees more in me than I see in myself, thank you for investing in me. On many occasions, you have given me the courage to keep going.

To my parents, John and Sandra Leysath, who have been amazing supporters in every facet of my life, thank you. What you have raised me to be is now being shared with the world. I know you raised me and my siblings to be great, but by placing us in the hands of Almighty God, you knew He would take us to places that would blow our minds. To my siblings, Alex, Joshua, Pertia, and Alexis—never stop believing and always keep pushing. There is more to your story, and others need your survival stories to give them confidence.

Dee with Rise2Write Publishing is simply amazing. Thank you for making this process smooth for me. You pushed me to bring this project to life and gave me the courage to create a truly life-changing piece. To all the community organizations, boards, and companies that trust in the God within me to inspire those who follow you, thank you.

To my amazing children, Jay and Kalise, I hope that my example inspires you to strive for all that you can be. And to my beautiful wife, Vinzanna, you are incredible! Thank you for supporting my wild dreams and ambitions to help everyone.

Whether it's preparing for a sermon, writing a book, or simply spending time with God, you allow me to pursue these passions without feeling guilty for not being present. There's so much more I could say, but I'll just say **THANK YOU!**

ABOUT JONATHAN LEYSATH

Jonathan Leysath is a pastor, entrepreneur, and financial professional who's passionate about helping people grow—in their faith, their finances, and their purpose. Ordained as an Elder under The Emmanuel Churches of Our Lord Jesus Christ, Inc., he has spent years serving in ministry, helping churches get stronger and more organized, and encouraging people to be intentional about their walk with God.

With 20 years of experience in the insurance and credit union industries, Jonathan knows firsthand how important financial stability is—especially for churches, businesses, and families trying to build something that lasts. He's worked with churches to improve their finances and operations, helping them be more effective in serving their communities.

Jonathan also gives back through leadership and mentorship, serving on several boards, including as a Trustee for his alma mater, Voorhees University. He believes in making an impact where it matters—whether it's in ministry, business, or helping the next generation succeed.

In ***Soaring on Purpose***, he challenges readers to stop just going through the motions and start making choices that truly align with God's plan. His message is simple: life gets better when you live on purpose.

www.ingramcontent.com/pod-product-compliance
Lightning Source LLC
Chambersburg PA
CBHW050652160426
43194CB00010B/1905